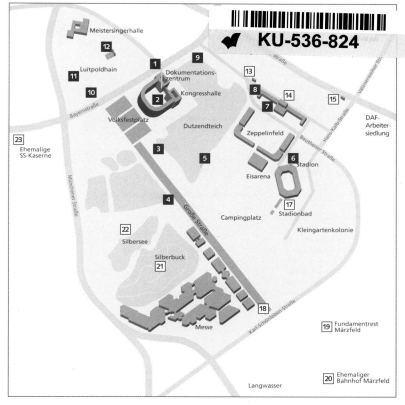

KU-536-824

Info Boards

Our suggested tour (approx. 2 hours) relates to info boards 1-12
and includes the most important areas of the Rally Grounds.

1 Documentation Centre
2 Congress Hall Courtyard
3 Funfair Area (Volksfestplatz)
4 Foundation Stone German Stadium
5 Dutzendteich Lake
6 Stadium
7 Zeppelin Grandstand
8 Zeppelin Field
9 Park-Café Wanner
10 Luitpold Hall
11 Luitpold Grove
12 Hall of Honour

13 Former Dutzendteich
   Railway Station
14 Zeppelin Grandstand Rear Wall
15 Transformer Building/
   DAF Worker's Accommodation
16 KdF Leisure Town
17 Stadium Swimming Baths
18 The Great Street
19 Remains of March Field
20 March Field Railway Station
21 Silberbuck Hill
22 Excavation for German Stadium/
   Silver Lake (Silbersee)
23 Former SS Barracks

PICTURE CREDITS

Archiv Foto Marburg: Front Cover, p. 35.
Bischof & Broel, Nürnberg: p. 57.
Deutsche Wochenschau GmbH: p. 3, 65.
Christine Dierenbach: p. 45.
Ernst Gortner: p. 58 b.
Geschichte Für Alle e.V. – Institut für Regionalgeschichte, Nürnberg:
    p. 6, 7, 9, 15, 16, 17 m., 40 b.r., 42, 43, 25, 27 t., 47 t., 31 t., 32, 33, 34,
    37, 38, 39, 59, 48, 49, 55 b., 60 b., 62, 65 t., 69 m., 69 b.
KZ-Gedenkstätte Flossenbürg: p. 27 b.
LiPopp/Stingl: p. 1.
Max Körner: p. 18 t.r., 22 t.r., 24 t.r., 30 t.r., 32 t.r., 40 t.r., 46 t.r.,
    48 t.r., 73 t.
**museen der stadt nürnberg, Dokumentationszentrum Reichsparteitags-
    gelände:** p. 16, 17 t., 17 b., 21 b., 23 t., 26.
Bestand Uwe von Poblocki: p. 14, 41, 21 t., 55 m.
Erika Sanden: p. 50, 51.
Stadtarchiv Erlangen: p. 55 t.
Stadtarchiv Nürnberg, Bild-, Film- und Tonarchiv: Back Cover t., p. 8, 10,
    29 t., 29 m., 40 b.l., 44, 19, 20, 23 b., 47 b., 31 b., 36, 56, 69 t., 70.
Stadtbibliothek Nürnberg: p. 11, 12, 13.
Sammlung Markus Urban: p. 66, 67.
wbg Nürnberg GmbH Immobilienunternehmen: p. 46, 52, 53.

The printing of this booklet has been sponsored
by the German Government's Art and Culture
Programme for the FIFA World Cup 2006™,
the German Government Representatives for Culture
and Media, the Bavarian Culture Fund and
the City of Nuremberg.

SANDBERG
VERLAG

© Sandberg Verlag
Wiesentalstraße 32
90419 Nürnberg

Information in English available at: Designer: Norbert Kühlthau, Nuremberg
www.geschichte-fuer-alle.de   Printing: Druckhaus Oberpfalz

info@geschichte-fuer-alle.de   Nuremberg 2006
Phone +49-911-307360
Fax +49-911-3073616   ISBN 3-930699-45-1 (German)
                                             ISBN 3-930699-47-8 (English)

Alexander Schmidt
Markus Urban

THE NAZI PARTY RALLY GROUNDS IN NUREMBERG

A Short Guide

Translated by John Jenkins

Historic Walks 4

Published by

Geschichte Für Alle e.V. – Institut für Regionalgeschichte
in cooperation with the City of Nuremberg

CONTENTS

4

The Former Nazi Party Rally Grounds

Walks Through History

■ Today, the huge expanse of ground in the south of Nuremberg, containing the relics of the monumental National Socialist architecture of the Nazi Party Rallies, is once again Nuremberg's largest sports and leisure complex – with lakes, parks, a football stadium, ice hockey arena, recreation area and motor-racing track. Whether they intend to or not, many local residents and visitors thereby come face-to-face with the National Socialist buildings and want to know more about the function and significance of the architecture and the ritual of the Rallies.

Nuremberg's role as the "City of the Party Rallies", the fact that the Nuremberg Laws were promulgated in the city and the Nuremberg Trials took place there after the war, mean that Nuremberg in particular has to come to terms with its history. The opening of the Documentation Centre Nazi Party Rally Grounds and its Study Forum in 2001 was an important milestone in this process. Since 2006 a comprehensive system of information boards has transformed the Rally Grounds area itself into a "place of learning", complementing the guided tours of the grounds that have been offered by *Geschichte Für Alle e.V.* for more than two decades.

This short guidebook from *Geschichte Für Alle e.V. – Institut Für Regionalgeschichte* and the *City of Nuremberg* incorporates the new information-boards system and facilitates the reader's own exploration of the former Rally Grounds. In addition, it provides compact background information on the Rallies.

We would like to thank all those who have assisted us with pictures, information and contacts. Our thanks also to the German Government's Art and Culture Programme for the FIFA World Cup 2006™, the German Government Representatives for Culture and Media, the Bavarian Culture Fund and the City of Nuremberg, who sponsored the printing of this booklet.

May 2006
Bernd Windsheimer

Geschichte für Alle e.V. –
Institut Für Regionalgeschichte
(History for Everyone –
Institute for Local History)

Nuremberg in the Nazi Period

Nazi Propaganda Shows
and a Place of Reckoning

The marching columns of the SA and SS at the 1934 Party Rally degraded the old town, using it as the stage for various Rally events. Nuremberg thus became a symbolic location in National Socialist Germany, known throughout the country and abroad as the "City of the Party Rallies". Photo 1934.

Perhaps more than any other city, Nuremberg was unambiguously linked to National Socialism. This was not just due to the Party Rallies and the marketing of this event by the media. The "Nuremberg Laws" from 1935 and Julius Streicher's anti-Semitic newspaper "The Stormtrooper" promoted Nuremberg's reputation as a Nazi city. Although the Nuremberg Trials meant that National Socialism was also brought to justice there, this was largely coincidence – the Palace of Justice and the nearby prison were two of the very few suitable buildings to survive the war. Many saw the trials as a disgrace and an unlawful act against the Germans. As a result they were misunderstood and cousidered a blot on the city's image.

Despite the fact that Nuremberg had firmly established itself as a modern industrial centre, to the Nazis it appeared as the appropriate setting for their parades: since the end of the 18th century the old part of the city within its completely-preserved walls had been considered the "treasure chest of the German Empire", Gothic architecture and half-timbered houses harked back to medieval greatness and Nuremberg's history afforded numerous links with the Holy Roman Empire of the German Nation. The marching Nazis saw themselves as a fitting complement to the old city.

Right: Hitler salutes the marching SA and SS on the Main Market Square. Magazine title 1934.

Far right: Nazi Propaganda unites the "Cathedral of Light" and Nuremberg Castle. Postcard 1937.

During the Party Rallies, Nuremberg was flooded with uniformed participants and visitors.
As a result, more and more people became acquainted with the city and thereby provided an important source of income. Photo mid-1930s.

Hitler was hostile to religion but he positioned himself in front of Our Lady's Church, using it to symbolize the greatness of the past. In numerous ways the propaganda of the swastika and other National Socialist symbols was combined with motifs from the old city.

Seen from this perspective the Rally Grounds appeared as the "New Nuremberg" i.e. as the answer to former greatness. What is largely forgotten is the significant amount of opposition to the Nazis in the "City of the Party Rallies", particularly from the labour movement. Several hundred Nuremberg citizens were imprisoned in Dachau and other concentration camps.

Aggression and violence, beginning in the 1920s in the regional Nazi movement led by Julius Streicher, were also part of the National Socialist period in Nuremberg. The Jews living in the city found the atmosphere there particularly hostile. To some extent this was due to the Party Rallies but above all to the primitive and loud-

The weekly newspaper "Der Stürmer" (The Stormtrooper), edited by schoolteacher and Gauleiter Julius Streicher, was the vehicle for an unparalleled anti-Semitic smear campaign. With special editions for the Party Rallies and mass subscriptions by whole sections of the Nazi movement, the paper made him into a millionaire.
Front pages of newspapers 1937 and 1939.

mouthed anti-Semitism of Streicher and his followers. The Nuremberg Laws, which prohibited marriages between Jewish and non-Jewish Germans, were promulgated by Göring at the 1935 Party Rally and greeted with a storm of approval by the Nuremberg National Socialists. The boycott of Jewish businesses in 1934, the destruction of the main Nuremberg synagogue even before the »Night of Broken Glass« in 1938 and the show trial of the head of the Nuremberg Jewish community Leo Katzenberger, who was accused of "race defilement" and sentenced to death (this verdict requiring the judge to bend even National Socialist Law), characterized Nuremberg's pronounced level of anti-Semitism and persecution of the Jews. Local Nazis also profited personally, making money from the later Aryanization. At least 2,373 Nuremberg Jews were victims of the Holocaust.

There were 21 defendants in the dock at the main trial, all representatives of the National Socialist state, with Hermann Göring sitting on the far left. The wide-ranging body of evidence presented the crimes of the regime to the world. Twelve of the accused were sentenced to death, three defendants were acquitted and the rest were given prison sentences ranging from ten years to life imprisonment. Photo 1945.

Horror and disillusionment marked the beginning of the post-war period in Nuremberg. After 12 years of Nazi rule the old city lay in ruins, there was hardly any functioning industry and many people had either died at the front or as a result of the air raids. Formely an advertisement for National Socialism, the "City of the Party Rallies" had now become an embarrassment and to a large extent people wanted to forget this part of its history. Initially, this attitude could be seen most clearly in the case of the trial of the major war criminals. Regarded as contributing to Nuremberg's soiled reputation, in reality a fair trial of major importance in world history had taken place at the start of a new era which gave more significance to the concept of international law. Although the trial had many shortcomings, the Allied Powers based proceedings on international

As a result of the air raids approx. 90 per cent of the old town was destroyed. The cityscape of Nuremberg and its reputation were ruined. Only decades later, following a period of reappraisal of its own history, could a more positive picture be presented to counter the image of Nuremberg as a Nazi city. Photo 1945.

law and judged the accused on the basis of their individual involvement. This was not a revenge trial.

At the level of municipal politics, a coming-to-terms with the Nuremberg Laws did not emerge until the 1990s. The opening of the city's "Street of Human Rights", recalling the United Nations Universal Declaration of Human Rights in 1948, reflects the new awareness. In addition, the Nuremberg International Human Rights Award has been presented every two years since 1995 and the Nuremberg Trials are now seen as a positive contribution to the city's history. Future plans include converting the historic Courtroom 600, scene of the trials, into a permanent exhibition accessible to the public.

The Nazi Party Rallies

Climax of the
National Socialist Festival Calendar

The NSDAP had already held two Party Rallies in Nuremberg during the Weimar Republic. These were on a much smaller scale but followed a similar pattern to those that took place during the Third Reich. The "March-Past" of SA and SS remained part of the programme in later years. Photo 1927.

The calendar of Nazi festivals drew much of its inspiration from Christianity and socialism. Examples are the national Harvest Festival (Reichserntedank) early in October as well as the May Day Rally in Berlin. Both were usually attended by more than a million people. The annual Nazi Party Rallies, which were held in September between 1933 and 1938, outshone all other mass celebrations in the Third Reich because they were continually expanded and soon stretched over an entire week. The regime presented them as a modern alternative to what they saw as the futile gatherings of the democratic parties of the Weimar Republic. In keeping with this idea, the sessions of the "NSDAP Convention" in the Luitpold Hall were intended to provide a framework for the week of events. But although Hitler's proclamation and closing speech were delivered here and other celebrity speakers appeared as well, the convention sessions were largely a decorative matter – there were no discussions, no decisions were made and instead of delegates, the audience consisted of more or less randomly chosen people. It was the large-scale marches and parades performed in Hitler's presence by various party and state organisations that formed the real focal point of the Party Rallies.

Propaganda minister Joseph Goebbels did not plan or organize the Party Rallies. This was the responsibility of "National Organization Leader" Robert Ley. Referred to as "Reich's Drunkard" in the vernacular, Ley controlled unlimited financial resources as leader of the national trade union (DAF), membership of which was compulsory for workers. Photo 1935.

Every year new elements were added to the festival week for the purpose of entertaining the participants e.g. sporting events on the so-called "Community Day" and the "Strength through Joy" (Kraft-durch-Freude, KdF) festival. Nazi hypocrisy became evident in their choice of name for the 1939 Rally – the "Party Rally of Peace" was cancelled just a few days before the German invasion of Poland which started World War II.

Documentation Centre

"Fascination and Terror" –
a Place to Study and Learn

The Documentation Centre in the north wing of the Congress Hall was designed by the Austrian architect Günter Domenig as a form of conscious architectural opposition to the structure of the Nazi building – its shape is a rejection of the use of right angles and symmetry. Computer simulation of the centre.

■ The Documentation Centre Nazi Party Rally Grounds is an architectural event: in particular the Study Forum in the roof section and the protruding flight of steps at the entrance are designed to counter the monumental style of the Nazi building. The centre's structure gives it an air of lightness, with the oblique angles, steel and glass opposing the massive granite façade of the hall. The steel spear which forms the entrance to the centre symbolically cuts through the Congress Hall like a dissecting knife. In this way, rather than subordinating itself to the National Socialist building, the Documentation Centre reverses the situation and makes the hall itself the central exhibit.

The Documentation Centre offers an exhibition that narrates the history and function of the Nazi Party Rallies and the Rally Grounds. This account is itself embedded in a more general history of National Socialism. Films, documents and other exhibits effectively illustrate what happened during the Nazi Party Rallies.

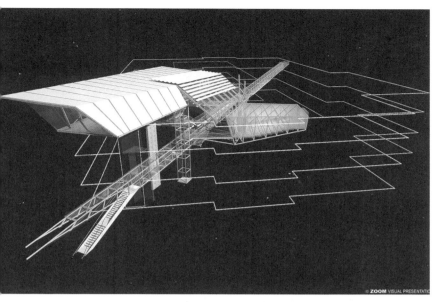

Film projections give a vivid impression of the colossal nature of the building plans for the Party Rally Grounds. A multilingual audioguide to the exhibition is also provided.

The Study Forum provides groups of visitors with a wide-ranging educational programme. In cooperation with various partners – including Geschichte Für Alle e.V. – the centre has been successful in offering a broad spectrum of themes for study and discussion.

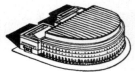

Congress Hall

The "first giant among the buildings
of the Third Reich"

**Nuremberg architect
Ludwig Ruff designed
the Congress Hall as a
gigantic construction
on the edge of the
Dutzendteich Lake, in
which it would then be
reflected. The founda-
tion stone was laid
during the 1935 Party
Rally. The "largest hall
in the world" was to be
erected on a horseshoe-
shaped ground plan.
Although the outside of
the hall reminds the
visitor of the Colosse-
um in Rome, its dimen-
sions were planned to
greatly exceed those of
the antique building.
Photo of a model of the
hall 1935.**

The Congress Hall on the shore of the
Dutzendteich Lake is one of the largest Nazi
buildings to survive the war. Its dimensions, the
natural stone façade and the use of an ancient
building as an architectural model are all important elements of the ideology that informed National Socialist architecture. One of the intended
effects of this style was to give the impression
that the "Third Reich" was to be a momentous
period in world history. In addition, Hitler believed
that the Germans suffered from an inferiority
complex and that viewing buildings of this nature
would improve their self-confidence. Thus the
practical function of the buildings had often
very little to do with their actual appearance.
Using granite for the façade was also deliberate:
it stood for the eternal character of the Congress
Hall. At the laying of the foundation stone in
1935, Hitler said that mankind would wonder for
a long time to come at this "first giant" among
the National Socialist buildings.

According to National Socialist propaganda,
the German stonemason produced high-quality
German workmanship. However, the large-scale
building sites of the Third Reich were organised
following ultramodern principles. The interiors
were constructed out of brick and reinforced con-

crete using the quickest building techniques. To reduce costs, granite for later building projects e.g. the German Stadium on the Rally Grounds, was also obtained from concentration camps. From 1938 onwards the SS set up camps especially for this purpose. Work on the Congress Hall began in 1935 and the 120-feet-high façade that can be seen today had already been built by 1938/39. Thus, contrary to the claim that is sometimes made, the granite used here did not come from the concentration camps of the National Socialists.

Hitler wanted the leading members of the Nazi Party (NSDAP), "the select of the German people", to gather in the interior of the Congress

Viewed from the inside, the Congress Hall would also have been an imposing structure, with room for at least 50,000 people. The semicircular area for participants was arranged around an altar-like speaker's platform. The flat, self-supporting roof with its huge skylight was intended to provide impressive lighting. Photo of a model of the hall interior from around 1940.

Hall every year for the Party Congress. A huge audience was to hear Hitler and other high-ranking Nazis and at the same time the large number of people present would prevent discussion and voting. Such democratic elements would have contradicted both the character of the NSDAP – as a party based on the Führer Principle – and the desired function of the congress. Debate was not to be the attraction in the hall but rather jubilation within the framework of a propaganda show. To achieve this effect, no expense would be spared. For instance, there were plans to build the world's biggest organ in the hall.

In spite of the enormous amount of manpower and building material involved, the Congress Hall remained incomplete. Following extensive work on the foundations, the shell of the building reached its present height in 1938 and by 1939 most of it had been covered in granite. Work continued during the war, partly with help from Soviet prisoners of war, but the outsized building was never finished. Neither the spectator stands inside nor the roof of the hall were ever

Construction of the Congress Hall proceeded rapidly. Two 1:1 scale wooden models provided a foretaste of façade (a) and interior (b). The models were also intended to impress Hitler when he visited Nuremberg. Postcard 1936 and photo 1938.

realised. The construction of the "greatest hall in the world" thus exemplifies the failure of National Socialism's architectural vision.

Attempts after 1945 to put the building to use – as a football stadium (in the 1960s) or as a shopping centre (in the 1980s) – came to nothing. The sheer size of the building caused problems for these projects and there were doubts about financial viability. In addition, moral questions arose about how such a building should be used in the future, given its intended function in Nazi Germany.

The interior of the Congress Hall today offers one of the most impressive examples of large-scale National Socialist architecture. A useful vantage point is the viewers' balcony in the Documentation Centre Nazi Party Rally Grounds.

The Great Street

From Nazi-Parade Area to Parking Lot

Two building sites: in the background, cranes and a wooden model of the Congress Hall façade. In the foreground, granite slabs ready for the Great Street. Many of the slabs remained unused up to the end of the war and were used as replacements during the later renovation. Photo 1937.

The so-called Great Street stretches between the Congress Hall torso and Nuremberg's modern Langwasser district. It was designed as a central axis of the Party Rally Grounds and in order to build it, Albert Speer had an embankment erected along this part of the Dutzendteich Lake. The street was to be over a mile long and 60 yards wide. It was conceived as a connecting line between the March Field – which was also under construction – and the Congress Hall and Luitpold Arena in the northern part of the Rally Grounds. Bordered on both sides by a low terraced area for standing spectators, the street was also to serve as a parade area for the German Army and the National Labour Service. Granite slabs of various colours were used to provide points of orientation for the marching soldiers. In addition, the surface of the slabs was roughened to avoid the embarrassment of participants slipping in wet weather. The Great Street was a priority project for Hitler and thus in 1937 he ordered that it be completed in time for the next Party Rally. However, it would still have remained unfinished for the 1939 Rally which had to be cancelled at short notice. The US Army "officially opened" the street, using it as a runway for small aircraft until 1968. This resulted in many of the slabs being dam-

NS propaganda liked to make references to Nuremberg's medieval past. Thus it was fitting that the Great Street created an optical connection to "old" Nuremberg. Photo 2006.

aged. At the beginning of the 1990s the City of Nuremberg had the street completely renovated at a cost of approx. six million euros so that it could continue to be used as a parking area for major events and for the nearby trade fair centre. On the side of the road nearest the wooded area some of the spectator stand steps, partly overgrown with grass, can still be seen today.

German Stadium

From "German Olympic Stadium"
to "Death Lake"

The horseshoe-shaped German Stadium was designed to hold 400,000 spectators. It was intended as the location for the "National Socialist Battle Games" during the Party Rallies and construction started in 1937. On completion it would have reached a height of 360 feet, making it by far the largest building on the Rally Grounds. However, as a result of the war, the project was never realised. Photo of a model of the stadium 1937.

█ The dimensions of Albert Speer's German Stadium would easily have exceeded the other Nazi buildings on the Rally Grounds. As the propaganda at that time put it, there would be room in the "world's largest stadium" for the entire population of Nuremberg. However, there was no well thought-out plan for the use of the building: no planning details for the sports facilities in the stadium interior have come down to us. The National Socialist "Battle Games" during the Rally week, combining militarism and athletics, would hardly have attracted that number of spectators. Due to the height of the auditorium – which would have given a very poor view of the events – it would have been necessary to provide the spectators with binoculars. The immensity of the planned stadium was matched only by the total failure to realize the project. For decades the foundation stone – laid by Hitler in 1937 and the stadium's only relic – remained relatively unnoticed in a small wooded area by the Great Street. The Silver Lake (Silbersee), formed when the large pit dug during the foundation work filled up with water, is still polluted today. Poisonous chemicals seeped into the lake when debris from the southern part of the bombed city was dumped on the nearby "Rubble Mountain" (Silberbuck).

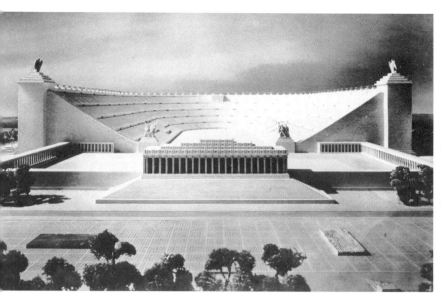

When the foundation stone for the German Stadium was laid on 9 September 1937, Hitler announced that the SA would be the organisers of the National Socialist "Battle Games". The foundation stone was removed in 2003 during the construction of a multi-store car park for the trade fair centre. It was brought back in 2006 as part of the information system. Photos 1937 and 1994.

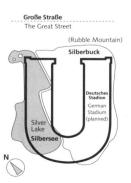

25

A life-size wooden model of part of the German Stadium auditorium was constructed in Hirschbachtal (near Oberklausen) to the east of Nuremberg. Albert Speer used the model to try out various angles of inclination for the spectator stands. Photo from around 1939.

Unusual steps were taken to prepare for the construction of the gigantic German Stadium and became part of Nazi propaganda. As there was not much to see of the actual stadium, Albert Speer exhibited models of the planned construction in a building in the Luitpoldhain and photos of the plans were published in newspapers and trade journals. On the building site itself a 1:1 scale model of the façade could be viewed by Hitler and other VIPs. Near Oberklausen, east of Hersbruck, sections of the spectator stand were constructed in wood. These projects served as architectural experiments but were also intended to give the impression of rapid progress and to eradicate any doubts about the realization of the plans. However, behind these façades there were major problems e.g. in obtaining and paying for the huge amount of granite required. To reduce costs, a deal was made with the SS, who accordingly set up their own German Earth and Stone Works Company to deliver building material for Speer's architectural projects. This meant that concentration camp prisoners were literally

Granite from Flossen-
bürg and other concen-
tration camps was
delivered to Nuremberg
for the construction of
the façade of the
German Stadium. How-
ever, only a large pit
was dug as part of the
preparations for one
section of the building.
This later filled up with
water to form the Silver
Lake (Silbersee). Photo
from 1937 of a model
of the stadium and
photo of the Flossen-
bürg quarry from around
1939.

worked to death by the SS in the quarries. From
1938 the SS even built four camps especially for
the purpose of granite production. The Natz-
weiler camp was set up in occupied France to
provide granite specifically for the German Stadium.

Before 1933

Recreation Area and
Laboratory for the Modern Age

For centuries the Dutzendteich area had been an important leisure park for the people of Nuremberg. A park restaurant was built on the lake shore in 1899. This later became Café Wanner.

The Dutzendteich Lake area had always been a favourite with day trippers. The Luitpold Grove, laid out for the Bavarian Jubilee Trade Exhibition of 1906, was a typical park of the period, with fountains, artistically arranged flower beds and a large exhibition hall. The zoo was opened near to the complex a short time later.

After WWI the area around the Zeppelin Field was upgraded. By 1928 a large allotments area had been added, as well as the stadium with its swimming pool, sports grounds for the general public, a "non-alcoholic" restaurant and a "sunbathing" café. The architecture from Otto Ernst Schweizer – flat roofs, reinforced concrete and clear-cut lineation – reflected the influence of the Bauhaus ideals.

The construction of the Nazi Party Rally Grounds destroyed Nuremberg's largest recreation site: the park gardens in the Luitpold Grove and on the banks of the Dutzendteich Lake, large wooded areas in the Langwasser region and even part of the Dutzendteich Lake itself made way for the dreary parade grounds, spectator stands and roads built for the Nazi Party Rallies.

The present-day folk festival area was formerly the site of Nuremberg's zoo. Built in 1912, the zoo was moved to Schmausenbuck when construction started on the Rally Grounds. Photo of the entrance 1930.

The stadium area with its swimming pool was opened in 1928, offering Nuremberg's citizens recreational and sporting facilities. The buildings were exemplary statements of modern architecture. Photo from around 1928.

Municipal Stadium

Hitler Youth and German Girl's League

To many young Germans the Nazi "experience" took on the appearance of an exciting adventure. However, the ideals of youth that Hitler presented to them in Nuremberg ("as quick as greyhounds, as tough as leather and as hard as Krupp steel"), led most of them directly to WWII. Many of those shown in this picture never returned from the war. Photo 1938.

■ With its blue steel struts and four floodlight masts the "Franconian Stadium" looks very modern from the outside. Only recently, 56 million euros was spent on the building, home of the local Nuremberg Football Club, to prepare it for the World Cup. The original "Municipal Stadium" was constructed on this spot in the 1920s: in those days it formed the centre of a modern recreational area, which included a public outdoor swimming pool, sports fields, allotments and a "non-alcoholic" restaurant. Although the style of the stadium and its adjacent buildings was closely linked to that of the "Bauhaus", which the National Socialists hated, it was used during the Party Rallies as the "Stadium of the Hitler Youth". Here, 50,000 members of the Hitler Youth and 5,000 members of the "German Girls' League" (BDM) paraded in uniform and listened to speeches from "Reich Youth Leader" Baldur von Schirach and Hitler – both used ideology to arouse their audience to fanaticism. From 1937 the speeches were followed by a ceremony to swear in the 18-year-old Hitler Youth boys as new party members.

Several thousand of those in the stadium had reached Nuremberg after a long march to the city from all over the country, which had lasted

The sports and recreational park around the Dutzendteich Lake, the work of Nuremberg's horticultural architect Alfred Hensel, was awarded a gold medal at the Olympic Games in Amsterdam in 1928. The stadium was designed by Otto Ernst Schweizer. With its modern main stand built of fair-faced concrete, it formed the focal point of the park area. It was placed under a preservation order after the war but collapsed "accidentally" during the conversion work for the "Franconian Stadium". Photo 1928.

several weeks. Nazi ideology strove to gradually alienate the youth from their families and at the same time place them under the command of state organizations. Accordingly, the Hitler Youth stayed in paramilitary camps during the Party Rally in order to prepare them for their future roles. Songs such as "The Flag is more than Death", sung as part of the "Day of the Youth" in the stadium, soon became reality: even during the very last days of the war in 1945, 16-year-old Hitler Youth boys died because the regime used them as cannon fodder.

Zeppelin Field

The "Community of the People"
and the "Cathedral of Light"

The Zeppelin Grand-
stand, completed in
1936, was supposed to
express the greatness of
antiquity through the
use of limestone, flame
bowls and colonnades.
Speer said he used the
Greek Pergamon Altar –
today in the Pergamon
Museum in Berlin – as
his model. Photo from
about 1937.

The Zeppelin Field, with its Grandstand designed by Albert Speer, was the most important
part of the Party Rally Grounds during the Third
Reich. The reference to Count Zeppelin, a pioneer
in the field of airship travel, dates back to 1909
when he caused quite a sensation by landing here
in one of his airships. The National Socialists first
used the field for their Party Rally parades in
1933. The decision to stage the event that year
had been taken at short notice and so only provisional stands with a large wooden eagle as national emblem in the background were erected.
In its completed form the Zeppelin Field and its
hastily-finished stone tribune were used for the
first time during the Party Rally of 1936. In the
following years most of the mass events during
the Party Rally week took place here: on differ-
ent days the Reich Labour Service and the Political Leaders held their parades and
march-past in front of

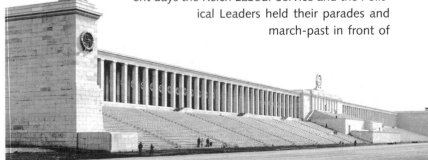

For the various march-pasts (here, the National Labour Service) Hitler always came down from the Grandstand. This direct eye-contact with the "Leader" was stylized into a central "Party Rally experience". Photo 1937.

the Grandstand. Furthermore, many events of the ever-expanding folk festival and the "Day of the Community", which was introduced in 1937, were held here. The German Armed Forces presented large-scale mock battles that were especially popular among the spectators – they were used to the military traditions of the former empire and most of them were gullible enough to believe in Hitler's repeated claims that the massive German rearmament would guarantee peace.

With space for well in excess of 100,000 uniformed men on the field and 80,000 spectators on the surrounding stands, the Zeppelin Field was the largest location for events on the Party Rally Grounds. However, it would have been exceeded by the German Stadium and the March Field,

Before the completion of the stone tribune in 1936, the events on the Zeppelin Field were staged in front of improvised wooden constructions. Photo 1933.

where most of the events would have been transferred.

It is clear that the Grandstand has not been preserved in its original size and shape. The middle section, with the speaker's pulpit installed for

Left and above: most participants and spectators could not see the entire crowd. This corresponded to National Socialist ideology – the individual was of no value, only the "Community of the People". Photos 1936 and 1938.

Hitler's speeches, remains more or less unchanged – the huge swastika on the top was the only part blown up by the U.S. Army in April 1945. However, in the late 1960s the City of Nuremberg decided to remove the colonnades on both sides, as well as the upper parts of the end pylons with the flame bowls. The decision was taken for economic and political reasons. Hastily erected by the Nazis, the building was already dilapidated and it did not seem reasonable to undertake the expensive renovation that would have been required. Furthermore, it was in keeping with the zeitgeist to dispose of another unpleasant piece of the past. This had already been done in the case of the Luitpold Arena.

The "National Socialist Games" combined militarism and sport. In 1937, the "Day of the Community" became part of the games, adding an extra day to the Party Rally week. Among other events, it included mass gymnastic exercises performed by members of the BDM (Nazi organisation for girls). However, National Socialism allowed women no political role. Photo 1938.

Standing on the steps of the Zeppelin Grandstand – the accessible middle part with the pulpit – we can see at close quarters the bad condition of many of the original stones. Many had already started to deteriorate during the war. As a result, awkward questions were raised at the time during sightseeing tours of the grounds – this was supposed to be an area constructed for a "Thousand Year Empire".

From the centre of the Grandstand a panoramic view is possible of the entire parade ground. Today the area is still enclosed in a rectangular fashion by the spectators stands but these are now partly covered by grass and weeds. At the time of the Party Rallies, the field lay completely open in front of the Grandstand: there were no fences, trees or sports grounds and no flat white building on the opposite side of the field from the stand. Through the open space where the building is today the party units and military battalions entered the field. Often the participants of the parades had to leave their camps in the middle of the night, as these were located up to ten miles away. After hours of marching, they still had to wait a long time for the arrival of the party elite and the beginning of the event. Nevertheless, for most people the ceremony of their own organization formed the central experience of the entire week. The members of the National Labour Service received a lot of applause for their exercises with spades and choir-like chanting. The various military manoeuvres of the Armed Forces were also very popular. For the low-ranking officers of the party (Political Leaders), rather unpopular among the Germans, there was compensation in the form of an evening celebration in the mystical glow of searchlights, similar to a religious service. Under-

"Army Day" on the Zeppelin Field formed the climax and end of the Party Rally week. So many people wanted to see the mock-battles with tanks and airplanes that later Rallies offered a morning and afternoon performance. In 1937, there were 550,000 orders for tickets, although the stands provided space for only 80,000 spectators. Photo 1935.

The SA's influence steadily decreased after the "coup" of 1934 and Hitler used Nuremberg to systematically strengthen the position of the military. Its generals inspected the march-past together with him from a small platform. Camera teams can be seen on both sides, shooting for the weekly newsreels and the film "Triumph of the Will". Photo 1934.

neath the "Cathedral of Light", Hitler annually assured them of their important role in the state. Even here, anti-Semitic propaganda was an indispensable part of his speeches.

The last Rallies were staged here in 1938. After the French surrendered in summer 1940, new preparations for another Party Rally got underway, but were soon stopped because of the continuous British resistance. The Third Reich in Nuremberg lasted only until April 1945, when the U.S. Army took over the Party Rally Grounds and then the entire city.

The American military erected sports grounds here after the war, calling the area "Soldiers Field". Later, it served as the venue for rock concerts and events of all kinds. Even the Rolling Stones have played there several times. The an-

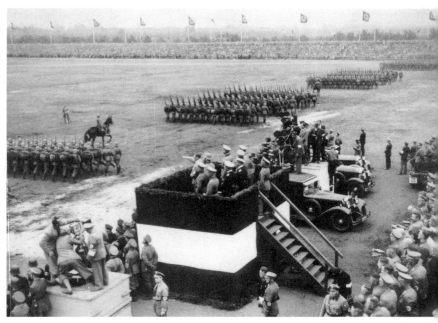

With the introduction of Speer's "Cathedral of Light" in 1936, the evening parade of the Political Leaders became virtually a sacred event. Hitler contributed to the creation of a mystical atmosphere by using vocabulary from the Bible. British ambassador Nevile Henderson wrote later that it felt like being in a "cathedral of ice". Photo 1937.

nual "Noris Ring" car race is also held here, hence the yellow marks on the asphalt. However, the rooms inside the Grandstand are no longer in use. They used to house a provisional exhibition dealing with the Party Rallies but this was later replaced by the new documentation centre.

For many years now, skaters, runners and tennis players have been using the public space around the Zeppelin Grandstand as a recreational area. But almost 70 years after the end of the last Nazi Party Rally, a convincing plan for the site, which would do justice to its historical importance and satisfy the town planners, has still not been put forward.

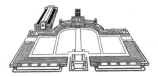

Luitpold Arena

The Party Congress and
the Consecration of the Flags

For the Bavarian Jubilee Trade Exhibition of 1906, the Luitpold Grove was laid out with exhibition buildings, footpaths and waterworks and presented as a typical park at the turn of the century. A monument to the dead of WWI, from the Nuremberg architect Fritz Mayer, was added in 1930. This was the only part of the old Luitpold Grove included in the Luitpold Arena of the National Socialists. Photo 1906 and postcard 1930.

The conversion of the Luitpold Grove into the Luitpold Arena started in 1933. This is the oldest part of the Party Rally Grounds but very little has survived. The area today, as in the period before 1933, takes the form of a large park. The monument erected to the dead of WWI provides the only orientation. It is now dedicated to the dead of both world wars and to the "Victims of Tyranny 1933-1945". The monument consists of an arcade, and a forecourt with flanking square pillars, each bearing a flame bowl. It was built during the era of the left-wing liberal mayor Hermann Luppe after more than a decade of discussion. Adolf Hitler liked the building and although neither finished nor inaugurated at the time, it already provided an ideological link for the meeting of the SA and SS held here during the 1929 Party Rally. From 1933 onwards it was used

">In 1933 the Nuremberg Structural Engineering Department, commissioned by the National Socialists, started to build the Luitpold Arena for the Cult of the Dead – a ceremony for the SA and SS. Almost all the exhibition buildings from 1906 were pulled down. Only the Luitpold Hall (a) remained, with an altered façade. The Congress Hall construction site can be seen behind the Luitpold Arena. Postcard 1936.

as the setting for the National Socialist Commemoration of the Dead. Instead of remembering the dead from WWI – these included Jewish citizens of Nuremberg – the Nazis had their own ceremony for the dead of their "Movement".

The park area in front of the monument was cleared and the fountains and numerous trees removed so that a pathway of granite slabs could be laid down the middle. This joined the war memorial at one end to the newly-built speaker's pulpit and rostrum with its imposing flag poles at the other. Three large swastika flags, each 80 feet high, dominated the rostrum. The Luitpold Arena and the Zeppelin Field were the only two complexes actually completed and used by the Nazis during the Party Rallies. A crucial factor in the decision to use the Luitpold Grove area was the large open space it would provide for mass gatherings – the view would not be obstructed by trees and

Hitler, Himmler and Lutze, in front of the war memorial. This area can still be seen today. In the background, the speaker's pulpit and VIP rostrum. The "Blood Flag" that the Nazis allegedly carried with them during the Hitler Putsch of 1923 is lowered in honour of the dead. On the ground in front of the flag is a large wreath. Photo 1934.

Right: Standing on the VIP rostrum next to the speaker's pulpit, Hitler used the "Blood Flag" to "consecrate" new SA standards.

there would be no fountains or flower beds to distract the audience. In addition, the speaker's platform and rostrum made it possible to present Hitler as the leader (Führer) and facilitated the appearance of mass formations in front of large numbers of spectators.

From 1933 onwards the National Socialists held their Commemoration of the Dead ritual in the Luitpold Arena. This became an established part of the ceremonies there. The ritual began with approximately 130,000 members of the SA and SS marching into the arena. Hitler then walked down the granite pathway in the middle between the assembled masses – from 1934 he was accompanied by SA leader Viktor Lutze and the head of the SS Heinrich Himmler – to the war memorial, where he bowed in front of a huge wreath. This was a theatrical presentation of Hitler as the lone, charismatic leader bearing sole responsibility for both the dead and (still) living

SA and SS assembled in front of Hitler at the 1934 Party Rally. Behind him the SA standards and guests of honour. At the other end of the complex the war memorial for the dead of WWI, degraded to just a part of the Luitpold Arena. Photo 1934.

members of the National Socialist Movement. The so-called "Blood Flag" from the 1923 putsch awaited Hitler at the war memorial. It was then carried behind him back to the VIP rostrum at the other end of the complex. There Hitler gave a short speech before "consecrating" SA standards. With a fixed stare, he would inspect the row of standard bearers, receive each bearer's report and then shake his hand before touching the standard with the "Blood Flag". In this ceremony and the walk to the war memorial – similar to a priest walking down a church aisle with his altar servers – Hitler played a religiously-charged role as saviour and messiah, with the "Blood Flag" functioning as a National Socialist relic. However, media-marketing played just as important a part in the success of the Rallies as the appeal to religious traditions and practices. Propaganda photographs taken from unusual perspectives – for instance, from the roof of the

Bayerische Jubiläums–Landes–Ausstellung Maschinenhalle.
NÜRNBERG 1906.

The Luitpold Hall was erected in 1906 for the Bavarian Jubilee Trade Exhibition. With a seating capacity of 16,000, it served as a civic exhibition and festival hall until the 1930s. Postcard 1906.

Albert Speer designed a new façade for the Luitpold Hall so that it would blend in with the Luitpold Arena. Flags played an important role in the theatricality of National Socialist architecture. Photo from after 1935.

war memorial – or the cinematic transformation of the Commemoration of the Dead ritual by using a special camera lift, made the "Roll Call of the Nazi Army" more impressive then it actually was.

The word "Reichsparteitag" ("Party Rally") refers to the meeting of a political party i.e. the Nazi Party (NSDAP). However, in the program of the Rallies this played a minor role and did not

correspond to National Socialist ideology – rather the Nazis saw themselves as a movement that had little in common with a democratic party and its practices.

Nevertheless, a party meeting did take place in the Luitpold Hall during the NSDAP Rally week. This "Party Convention" ("Parteikongress"), as it was officially called, did not provide an opportunity to discuss policy but instead served to promote externally the Nazi Party's self-image and internally the motivation of its members. The messages sent out from the congresses were simple. As Rudolf Hess said at the 1938 Rally: "The German people know that everything the Führer does is right."

The Luitpold Hall was destroyed in WWII. The area today is used as a parking lot.

In 1959 the City of Nuremberg reconverted the Luitpold Arena into a park. Suppressing the past by demolishing its architectural legacy characterised the early decades of the post war period. The annual Classic-Open-Air concert in the Luitpold Grove, first held here in 2000, can be seen as an attempt to reappropriate a leisure park area that had been destroyed by the National Socialists. Photo 2002.

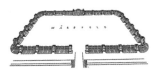

The March Field

War Games

The March Field Towers that had been built during the Nazi period were blown up in 1966 and 1967 to make way for a new residential area. Photos 1966.

■ The March Field was planned as the largest parade area on the Rally Grounds. Almost 1,000 yards wide and over 600 yards long, it was positioned at the end of the Great Street so as to form an architectural conclusion to the Rally Grounds area. On completion of the complex, the mock battles of the Armed Forces were to be transferred there from the Zeppelin Field. These events took place on the "Day of the Armed Forces" and were the annual highlight of the Rally week, attracting many spectators.

The name March Field alludes to Mars, the Roman god of war and also to March 1935 when compulsory military service was reintroduced in Germany in defiance of the Versailles Treaty.

In the planning for this part of the Rally Grounds the influence of contemporary and ancient architecture was present as well as the artist's personal vision. At first Albert Speer envisaged having an imperial eagle placed in the axis of the Great Street. But sculptor Josef Thorak took over the design and planned an ensemble of male figures in heroic pose with a 39-feet-high statue of the goddess Victory in the middle. Victory in battle against a background in which the individual counts for nothing – this was the real aim of National Socialism and on the March Field it was expressed architecturally.

Work on the March Field started in 1936. It was intended for parades and manoeuvres of the Armed Forces and would have been enclosed by spectator stands, fortified towers and hundreds of large swastika flags. Photos: model of the building in 1936 and after 1938.

Only a few parts of the March Field foundations can still be seen today – at the end of the Great Street that leads into the Langwasser district of Nuremberg. The rest has been replaced by the district's northern section.

The Camp Area

Drill and Camp Romanticism

Members of the Hitler Youth marching out of their camp in Langwasser. The propaganda portrayed "camp life" as an exciting communal experience. It was particularly attractive to children and young people. Photo 1937.

The provision of mass accommodation was from the very beginning one of the most important tasks facing the organisers of the Party Rallies. At first schools, sports halls and other buildings were used to house the participants. From 1935 additional accommodation was provided by a "city" of tents and barracks, laid out systematically in the undeveloped Nuremberg-Langwasser area. A complex of streets and railway stations was erected and the area had its own sewage system and power lines. However, the so-called "camp railway station" for the March Field was not ready for use until the last Party Rally in 1938. This meant that the participants had to

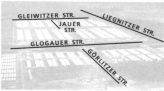

The street pattern today still allows the visitor to make out the various sections of the camp area.

The participants at the Rallies were accommodated in huge camps consisting of tents or barracks. SA, SS, the National Labour Service, the Hitler Youth (HJ) and other groups each had a demarcated camp area with its own gate. Also called the "Reich-Encampment", military drill was here the order of the day. Postcard from 1939 and photo 1934.

march for hours to get from their remote accommodation to the ceremonies in the inner city.

The SA camp consisted of about 400 tents, each with room for 250 men, so that 100,000 participants could be accommodated, making it the biggest camp on the Rally Grounds. The SS, the National Labour Service and the Hitler Youth were housed in smaller camps. The installation of the infrastructure and erection of the tents began weeks before the start of a Party Rally.

Camp life was not just a communal experience, it was also an exercise in military discipline and drill. Getting up at the crack of dawn, marching with a heavy backpack to Rally ceremonies, taking part in the evening military tattoo and accepting the restrictions on individual freedom of movement were part and parcel of life in the camp. For instance, the rigid camp regulations prohibited members of the Hitler Youth from going off on their own to the inner city. Given these background details, one is justified in viewing the Party Rallies as providing the opportunity to train men for war. The city of tents was erected for the last time in 1939 but not used – the Rally was cancelled at short notice due to the invasion of Poland. In WWII the SS camp became a forced-labour camp and the SA camp was turned into a POW camp for about 30,000 soldiers. For most of the prisoners new barracks were provided. Watchtowers and a double barbwire fence were erected to prevent escapes.

In the second half of 1941, at least 600 of the Soviet prisoners of war died as a result of hard labour and malnutrition. In an operation carried out by the Nuremberg Gestapo, Red Army officers who appeared suspicious in any way were rounded up and transported to Dachau Concen-

With the outbreak of war, the Party Rallies camp area became a prisoner-of-war camp for 30,000 soldiers from various countries. The Soviet prisoners-of-war, some of whom were forced to live in tents, were treated so badly that many died. This was in keeping with National Socialist ideology. Photos from the early 1940s.

Soviet prisoners of war on the way to work. With the exception of the officers, all prisoners of war were made to work. Some were accommodated in barracks provided by the various firms. Photo from the early 1940s.

tration Camp, where they were immediately murdered by the SS. As well as Polish POWs, (from 1939) and the Soviet prisoners (from 1941), Belgian and French (1940/41), Italian (from 1943/44) and finally, American officers and soldiers were imprisoned in Langwasser. On 17/18 April 1945 the US Army liberated the prisoners and the camp then served as an internment area for Germans suspected of being involved in National Socialist crimes. They were arrested, brought to the camp and questioned there. Generals, leading politicians and many others were imprisoned in Langwasser. Administration of the internment camp was handed over to the Germans in 1946. It was closed in 1949.

In the later post-war period, the barracks were still being used because of a lack of housing at the time. They formed the "Langwasser Housing Estate in Nuremberg" and were occupied by refugees and people who had been expelled from their homeland. Today's Langwasser district also has its roots in a camp for displaced persons (DPs) – including many people from Eastern Europe –

who had lost their homes and were now searching for better prospects and a new place to live. This so-called "Valka Camp" – named after a town located on the border between Estonia and Latvia – was set up in 1946 on a part of the former camp area that had been used during the Party Rallies. For a time 4,500 people were housed here in what later came to be known as the "Federal Transit Camp for Foreigners". The camp was closed in 1960. It was succeeded by the Federal Ministry for Migration, which was set up initially in the neighbouring town of Zirndorf but is now located in Nuremberg.

Faced by a growing housing shortage, there was great interest on the part of the City of Nuremberg and its housing department to build houses and apartments on the former Rally Grounds camp area. After protracted negotiations, work on the new district of Langwasser started in 1957. Gradually the various zones of the former Rally Grounds camp area became part of the housing estate. Some of the district's

Between 1945 and 1960 the Party Rallies camp area in Langwasser was used as an internment camp, a camp for displaced persons, a refugee camp and as a "Federal Transit Camp for Foreigners". Photo from late 1950s.

WOHNSIEDLUNG - NBG. LANGWASSER

Geschäftshaus · Lewandovski

Teil der Siedlung

Geschäftshaus · Drogerie

Geschäftshaus · Konsum

The first residents of the new district of Langwasser had to set up home in the barracks that had been used during the Party Rallies. Until 1960 the "Langwasser Housing Estate, Nuremberg" was populated by displaced persons and Silesian refugees. Postcard from the 1950s.

residential areas boast sophisticated architecture and are exemplary realizations of contemporary town-planning. Although Langwasser is now Nuremberg's largest district, its development is still continuing.

The laying of the foundation stone for the Langwasser district on 29 March 1957 marked the beginning of the largest extension of the city of Nuremberg. Today 35,000 people live there. Photo 1957.

INFO BOARDS
13 15 16 23

Surrounding Buildings

Infrastructure and Logistics

In 1937 the leisure organisation Strength-through-Joy (Kraft-durch-Freude, KdF) opened the KdF town, which consisted of five wooden halls, the largest being the "Franconia Hall". Together they could hold 7,500 people. This folk festival with its beer tent atmosphere was a fixed event in the Rally week programme. Photo 1937.

■ The remains of various buildings in an extensive area surrounding the Nazi Party Rally Grounds are present-day reminders of the infrastructure that came into being as a result of the Party Rallies. The March Field Railway Station was built to serve as the "Rallies Camp Railway Station", enabling the German National Railway to cope with the large numbers of participants and spectators who came to Nuremberg from all over Germany. In addition, the Dutzendteich, Fischbach and Zollhaus stations were redesigned and expanded. Thus in 1938, regular trains could bring 700,000 spectators to the city and the special trains 560,000 participants. The extension of the four-lane Regensburger and Münchener Streets enabled the eastern and western sections of the Rally Grounds to link up with the motorway.

The ordinary participant was accommodated in one of the huge tent camps. The camp area today forms part of the Langwasser district. For "the Führer's guests of honour" from Germany and abroad a Nazi Party guesthouse was built opposite the main railway station. The German Labour Front erected a camp in Regensburger Street for workers employed in the construction of the Rally Grounds. There were 14 large buildings to accommodate the workers and a hall/kitchen complex.

The KdF town was totally destroyed during an air raid in August 1942. Today the area in Valznerweiher Street is used as training grounds by Nuremberg's Football Club.

Huge crowds at Dutzendteich Railway Station after it had been expanded in 1934. Today the building houses a restaurant. Photo 1934.

The transformer station in Regensburger Street was designed by Albert Speer. It provided the power supply for the Rally Grounds and made the "Cathedral of Light" ceremony possible. The building today is home to a fast-food chain outlet. Photo 1937.

The August-Meier-Heim, a home for senior citizens, is located today in the vast "Deutsche Arbeitsfront" (DAF) workers' accommodation complex in Regensburger Street. Photo 1937.

In 1936 the Nazis opened a guesthouse next to the Grand Hotel in front of the main railway station. There were 142 beds for "the Führer's guests of honour" from Germany and abroad. Photo 1937.

The barracks building in Bayern Street was officially opened in 1939 and provided accommodation for the SS. This was one of the largest Nazi constructions of its kind and for decades after the war was used by the US Army. Since 1996 it has housed the Federal Office for Migration and Refugees. Aerial photo 2001.

The "Strength-through-Joy" town was located on the present-day training grounds of Nuremberg Football Club in Valznerweiher Street but it did not survive the war. In wooden folkloric halls, originally built in Berlin for the 1936 Olympics and later transported to Nuremberg, the Rally participants could spend what little free time they had enjoying traditional festive events in a beer-tent atmosphere.

In 1939 the huge SS barracks complex in Bayern Street was finally occupied, the so-called "Gateway to the Party Rallies". The monumental style of the barracks' architecture was the work of Franz Ruff. It was meant to symbolize power relations in the Nazi state. After 1945 it was used for decades as a barracks by the US Army. Since 1996, following extensive alterations, it has housed the Federal Office for Migration and Refugees.

March Field Railway Station

The Last Station before the
Extermination Camp

The Gestapo organised two deportations of Nuremberg and North Bavarian Jews from the March Field railway station to the concentration camps of Jungfernhof and Izbica. Almost 2,000 people were deported, only a few survived. Some of the March Field towers can be seen in the background of the picture. Photo 1941.

The former March Field railway station lies some distance away from the large relics of the former Nazi Party Rally Grounds and is without doubt one of its most impressive areas. The building was designed to acccommodate masses of people, with a 70-yards-long underpass leading to eight platforms. The station was used for the fast and last time during a Party Rally in 1938 and was never completed. Part of the northern section of the main building survived and is a reminder of how imposing the finished construction would have been. Neglected for years, the area is now overgrown and dilapidated.

The March Field railway station was opened in 1938 to transport Party Rally participants and spectators to the Rally Grounds in the southeast of Nuremberg and to the March Field area. It was only partly completed by the beginning of the war. A few parts of the façade have survived, as well as some stairways and platforms. Photo of a model 1938.

The March Field railway station and a hutted camp nearby were used for two deportations of Jews to concentration camps in Eastern Europe. The deportations, on 29 November 1941 and 24 March 1942, sent almost 2,000 people to their deaths. The senior SS officer and head of police Benno Martin planned the operation so that it would proceed inconspicuously and at the same time give the victims the impression that there was a chance of surviving. Although the Jews had to hand over their valuables to the German authorities and were then informed that the state had taken away all their property rights, they were allowed to take luggage and food with them into the trains. Even the old and the infirm had to carry their luggage several miles from the collection camp in Langwasser to the departure point near the March Field railway station. As they did so, the Jews were filmed, photographed and mocked by the guards. From the 940 Nuremberg Jews deported only 17 survived.

Most of the 10,000 soldiers held in the Langwasser prisoner-of-war camp were brought there by train, arriving at the March Field railway station.

Riefenstahl and Speer

Two Careers

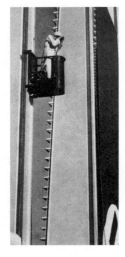

A trademark of Leni Riefenstahl's innovative technique as a director was the unusual camera positions, such as those facilitated by this specially-designed elevator on a flagpole. Such features enabled her "documentaries" to achieve an aestheticizing way. Photo 1934.

■ The rapid rise of Leni Riefenstahl and Albert Speer during the Third Reich followed a similar pattern. They made careers for themselves early, were not party members and both stood outside the traditional hierachies as artists specially commissioned by Hitler. Furthermore, their success was closely related to the Party Rallies.

The actress and director Riefenstahl had established contact with the highest level of the NSDAP in 1932 and Hitler commissioned her to film the Party Rally of 1933. The result, a one-hour film called "Victory of Faith", was shown in cinemas all over Germany a few months later, with considerable support from the regime's propaganda machine. However, after the alleged SA putsch of 30 June 1934 "Victory of Faith" was never again shown during the "Third Reich" because it had given such a prominent role to the fallen SA leader Ernst Röhm. Instead, Riefenstahl was asked to produce an even bigger, more expensive film of the 1934 Party Rally. With a crew of 120 people and a generous budget, she shot "Triumph of the Will". This is still the world's best-known propaganda film. Riefenstahl condensed the Party Rally week into three artificial "film days", changed the chronological order of events and contributed herself to the forma-

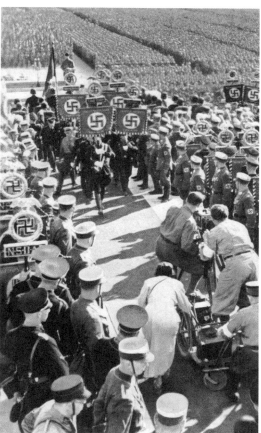

Until her death in 2003, Riefenstahl insisted that she had presented the Party Rallies in a neutral way e.g. by pointing to the fact that she had never used a spoken commentary in her films. However, in reality she had produced a work of propaganda which presented the Party Rally as a seemingly perfect theatrical performance, underlining the effect by adding catchy marches and music from Richard Wagner. Some scenes were even re-shot in the studio. Photo 1934 and film stills from "Triumph of the Will".

Speer's architectural style was inspired by Greek antiquity and sought to both over-whelm and elevate the beholder at the same time. The rear of the Zeppelin Grandstand shows his attempt to create an atmosphere of timelessness through the use of natural stone, red swastika flags and the total exclusion of any other architectural ornamentation. Photo 1938.

tion of the "Hitler myth". Already in the first scene, the dictator's arrival in Nuremberg is turned into a Messianic appearance – as it emerges out of the clouds, Hitler's plane is bathed in sunlight. In 1935 she directed a third Party Rally film, "Day of Freedom". Just 18 minutes long, it glorified rather than documented the appearance of the military at the Rally that year.

As a young student of architecture in Berlin, Albert Speer had also made contact with the National Socialists shortly before the party came to power. His first important work for the NSDAP was to provide decorative "stage sets" for the big May Day Parade in Berlin in 1933. Satisfied with the result, Hitler gave Speer the task of constructing most of the large parade grounds in the country and later, the main responsibility for modernizing the capital, Berlin. From 1934 onwards, the 29-year-old Speer was also put in charge of the Party Rally Grounds in Nuremberg – with the exception of the Convention Hall, which was the work of architect Franz Ruff. Speer's most important construction in Nuremberg was the Zeppelin Field with its Grandstand. However, the March Field and the German Stadium (which was never started) were also tasks assigned to Speer's office. Even providing the ornamental settings for individual events was part of his duties. This involved more than decorating façades in the old town with flags and laurel wreaths: it was also Speer's idea to give the evening event ("Hour of Consecration") of the Political Leaders an almost sacred atmosphere by creating a "Cathedral of Light" out of 150 anti-aircraft searchlights.

As in the case of Riefenstahl, Speer's role was not limited to that of the apolitical artist: in spring 1942 Hitler asked him to take over the Armaments Ministry. During the last three years of the war, Speer cleverly managed the German weapons industry and got deeply involved in the exploitation of forced labour from the concentration camps. Because of his role here, the full extent of which was not even fully exposed at the time, Speer was put on trial by the International Military Tribunal in Nuremberg and sentenced to 20 years' imprisonment in 1946. After his release, he started a second career as a bestselling author. Again, like Leni Riefenstahl, he was keen to create his own autobiographical myth and it is only during the last few years that the weaknesses of this account have come to the surface.

Nazi propaganda liked to present Hitler as the inspired artist-politician whose sketches provided the original ideas for the buildings on the Party Rally grounds. Photo 1938.

Foreign Perspectives

Diplomats, Journalists and Tourists

It was a matter of prestige for the Nazis to induce as many foreign diplomats as possible to attend the Party Rallies as honorary guests. A special "diplomatic train", which consisted of sleeping cars with small apartments, brought them from Berlin to Nuremberg, where they took part in the most important events. Photo 1937.

As soon as the National Socialist regime had successfully stabilized its power in Germany, it began to direct the propaganda messages of the Party Rallies abroad. Thus, during the 1935 "Party Rally of Freedom", Hitler announced an anti-Bolshevist objective. In the following years the Nazis used the Rallies to try and convince the world that there were only two possibilities for the democratic countries: Bolshevist chaos or a state of "order" symbolized and guaranteed by fascism. Consequently, the regime invited an increasing number of foreigners to the Rallies, to get them to know the "new" Germany. This was done to win over professors, journalists and opposition politicians, who would then promote understanding and agreement with Nazi Germany in their home countries. In particular, the Nazis wanted to impress the British representatives because they saw the country as a potential ally. Other foreign guests were courted for economic reasons – the regime hoped to conclude lucrative business or weapons deals with them. Each year about 250 foreign VIPs were invited as "honorary guests of the Leader" and granted various privileges: travel expenses were covered and hotel rooms paid for, free tickets issued for many Party Rally events, and there were also excursions and

Sir Nevile Henderson was the first British ambassador to attend a Party Rally – in 1937, shortly after assuming office. The picture shows him on the Zeppelin Grandstand during the Parade of the National Labour Service. Next to him Hermann Goering, through whom he unsuccessfully tried to influence Hitler's political decisions. Photo 1938.

personal meetings with high-ranking party celebrities. Some of the important guests of honour were seated in cars in Hitler's motorcade and were driven for an hour through the fanatical cheering crowds. The idea was to let them experience at close quarters the apparently unconditional support of the Germans for their leader.

Other foreigners came simply out of curiosity or sympathy to National Socialism and met their own costs. The Party took great care to present an acceptable public image to such guests, providing them with special guides proficient in the relevant language(s).

THE RIVAL MASTERSINGERS OF NUREMBERG

A British daily newspaper caricatured Hitler's appearance at the 1934 Rally as a performance of Wagner's "Mastersingers" opera. While Hitler sings his "song of praise" in front of a contented audience, a ragged figure backstage symbolises the coming winter with its economic problems. Daily Express, 6 September 1934.

During the early years of the Third Reich, the organizers did not manage to attract a large number of foreign diplomats from Berlin to Nuremberg. In the beginning, only Fascist Italy sent its ambassador, while most of the other states were either represented by an insignificant chargé d'affaires or not at all. This was especially true for the major powers: in summer 1936 the British Foreign Office noted that in no other country in the world did the government try to persuade diplomats to attend an event so far away from the capital and which "involves nearly a week's

The American weekly magazine "Life", like many foreign publications, fell victim to the fascination of mass aesthetics. It printed propaganda photos from Nuremberg largely without critical comment. Life 1936.

An effective stand against National Socialism was taken by the British weekly newspaper "Picture Post". The photos of the Nazi leaders published in the paper revealed them as hateful aggressors – the pictures had been rejected by the German censor. The ironic use of quotations and the inclusion of pictures of anti-Semitic violence strengthened the paper's message. Picture Post 1938.

absence in an obscure provincial town." However, with the emergence of appeasement politics, opinions changed quickly. Already in 1937, the ambassadors of France and Great Britain attended the Party Rally. The USA followed one year later.

The way in which foreign visitors and journalists perceived the Nuremberg events depended very much on the political attitudes they brought with them. Some considered the mandatory Labour Service an institution that should be introduced in their home countries, while many others were impressed by the cheering crowds and the glamorous mass performances. However, most foreign visitors also noticed the ever-present spirit of fanaticism, racial hatred and militarism, realistically interpreting such features as harbingers of a new war.

SERENADENHOF
NÜRNBERG

Stuyvesant

MUSIKALISCHER SOMMER
AUF DER ROMANTISCHEN FREILICHTBÜHNE

After 1945

A Difficult Inheritance

In the 1970s the Zeppelin Field was already a venue for concerts. A performance by Bob Dylan provided perhaps the greatest contrast to the aesthetics of National Socialist ceremonies: the stage was opposite the Zeppelin Stand, so that the audience of 70,000 had a good view of the concert from above. In both dress and behaviour this generation also distanced itself markedly from the uniform centralized state of the "Third Reich". Photo 1978.

■ When the US Army captured Nuremberg on 20 April 1945, a large part of the "City of the Party Rallies" had been destroyed. Nuremberg was presented with new challenges and in the climate of rebuilding and denazification many sought to repress the past. Consequently, people were not ready to come to terms with the Nuremberg Trials (which lasted until 1949), just as they were reluctant to address themselves to the architectural remains on the former Rally Grounds near the Dutzendteich Lake. While the Luitpold Arena was reconverted into a park, various suggestions were made about the future use of the Congress Hall e.g. conversion into a stadium or shopping centre. Initially, no information about the history of the Rally Grounds was available at these locations nor around the Zeppelin Stand, which had now become the venue for concerts and car races and a practice area for sport enthusiasts. When the City of Nuremberg opened the small exhibition "Fascination and Terror" inside the Zeppelin Stand in 1985, it became clear that there was a great deal of public interest in the history of the Rally Grounds area. However, the exhibition remained provisional and underfinanced, forced to close in the winter months because of lack of heating. Regular tours of the area were first

The US Army used the former Rally Grounds for a long time after the war. Until 1968 the Great Street served as a runway and the Zeppelin Field was turned into a sports ground. The field was handed back to the City of Nuremberg at the beginning of the 1990s. Photo 1960s.

Various suggestions were made for alternative uses of the Congress Hall torso, including convertion into a football stadium. An architectural model helped the city council get an impression of what the completed stadium would look like. Photo 1955.

offered by *Geschichte Für Alle e.V.* bringing a considerable number of visitors from Nuremberg and beyond to the Rally Grounds. In 1995, with the 50th anniversary of the end of WWII, a process of public discussion began on the subject of how best to inform and educate those visiting the former Rally Grounds. This resulted in the opening of the Documentation Centre Nazi Party Rally Grounds in autumn 2001. A bilingual information system was added in May 2006 – a set of 23 picture boards, erected at various locations on the former Rally Grounds area, provides information for visitors and enables them at the same time to explore the whole area for themselves.

The vast architectural remains of the Nazi period in Nuremberg are part of Germany's national heritage and the City of Nuremberg is aware that it bears the main responsibility for the former Rally Grounds. In 2005 the council voted unanimously to issue a set of guidelines for the future use of this historical site and its buildings, in which the city pledges itself to a continual examination of its dealings with the former Rally Grounds. This statement came in the wake of a competition for new ideas in urban development that had been held in summer 2001. It brought to light the fact that there is no overall planning concept dealing with the everyday use of the area which also does justice to its historical importance.

Future dealings with the Rally Grounds area will be a matter of engaging in open dialogue with the public. The buildings that bear witness to the Nazi period must be preserved as monuments and historical sources so that coming generations can develop their own ways of coming to terms with this heritage.

BURDEN, HAMILTON T.: The Nuremberg Party Rallies: 1923-1939, London 1967.

BURLEIGH, MICHAEL: The Third Reich. A New History, London 2000.

CENTRUM INDUSTRIEKULTUR (ED.): Kulissen der Gewalt. Das Reichsparteitagsgelände in Nürnberg, München 1992.

CULBERT, DAVID/ LOIPERDINGER, MARTIN: Leni Riefenstahl's "Tag der Freiheit". The 1935 Nazi Party Rally Film, in: Historical Journal of Film, Radio and Television 12 (1992), p. 3-38.

DEUTSCHMAN, LINDA: Triumph of the Will. The Image of the Third Reich, Wakefield 1991.

DIETZFELBINGER, ECKART/ LIEDTKE, GERHARD: Nürnberg – Ort der Massen. Das Reichsparteitagsgelände. Vorgeschichte und schwieriges Erbe, Berlin 2004.

DOOSRY, YASMIN: „Wohlauf, lasst uns eine Stadt und einen Turm bauen…" Studien zum Reichsparteitagsgelände in Nürnberg, Tübingen 2002.

EVANS, RICHARD J.: The Coming of the Third Reich, London 2003.

EVANS, RICHARD J.: The Third Reich in Power 1933-1939, London 2005.

GENTILE, EMILIO: The Struggle for Modernity, Westport 2003.

GESCHICHTE FÜR ALLE E.V. (HRSG.): Nürnberg-Langwasser. Geschichte eines Stadtteils, Nürnberg 1995.

GESCHICHTE FÜR ALLE E.V. (HRSG.): Geländebegehung. Das Reichsparteitagsgelände in Nürnberg, Nürnberg ⁴2005.

GRIFFIN, ROGER: International Fascism. Theories, Causes and the New Consensus, London 1998.

HENDERSON, NEVILE: Failure of a Mission. Berlin 1937-1939. New York 1940.

JASKOT, PAUL B.: The Architecture of Oppression. The SS, Forced Labor and the Nazi Monumental Building Economy, London 2000.

KAROW, YVONNE: Deutsches Opfer. Kultische Selbstauslöschung auf den Reichsparteitagen der NSDAP, Berlin 1997.

KERSHAW, IAN: The "Hitler Myth". Image and Reality in the Third Reich, Oxford 1987.

KERSHAW, IAN: Hitler. 1889-1936: Hubris, London 2001.

KERSHAW, IAN: Hitler. 1936-1945: Nemesis, London 2001.

KERSHAW, IAN: Popular Opinion and Political Dissent in the Third Reich: Bavaria 1933-1945, Oxford ²2002.

KERSHAW, IAN: Making Friends with Hitler. Lord Londonderry and the Roots of Appeasement, London 2004.

KIESSLING, FRIEDRICH/ SCHÖLLGEN, GREGOR (HRSG.): Bilder für die Welt. Die Reichsparteitage der NSDAP im Spiegel der ausländischen Presse, Köln 2006.

MILLFULL, JOHN (HRSG.): The Attractions of Fascism. Social Psychology and Aesthetics of the "Triumph of the Right", New York 1990.

MOSSE, GEORGE L.: The Nationalization of the Masses. Political Symbolism and Mass Movements in Germany from the Napoleonic Wars through the Third Reich, New York 1975.

OGAN, BERND/ WEIẞ, WOLFGANG W. (HRSG.): Faszination und Gewalt. Zur politischen Ästhetik des Nationalsozialismus, Nürnberg 1992.

REICHE, ERIC G.: The Development of the SA in Nürnberg, 1922-1934, Cambridge 1986.

REICHEL, PETER: Der schöne Schein des Dritten Reiches. Faszination und Gewalt des Faschismus, Wien 1991.

SHIRER, WILLIAM L.: Berlin Diary. Journal of a Foreign Correspondent 1934-1941. New York 1941.

WILSON, WILLIAM JOHN: Festivals and the Third Reich, Hamilton 1994.

WHITE, JOHN BAKER: Dover Nürnberg Return, London 1937.

WYKES, ALAN: The Nuremberg Rallies, New York 1970.

URBAN, MARKUS: Die Konsensfabrik. Funktion und Wahrnehmung der NS-Reichsparteitage, 1933-1941 (not yet published).

ZELNHEFER, SIEGFRIED: Die Reichsparteitage der NSDAP. Geschichte, Struktur und Bedeutung der größten Propagandafeste im nationalsozialistischen Feierjahr, Nürnberg ²2002.

**Already published
in this series:**

(A) Documentation Centre
(Dokumentationszentrum)
Bayernstraße 110

(B) Congress Hall
(Kongresshalle)
Courtyard and Gallery

(C) The Great Street
(Große Straße)
From Congress Hall to Langwasser district

(D) German Stadium
(Deutsches Stadion)
Today: Silver Lake (Silbersee) and Silberbuck

(E) Municipal Stadium
(Städtisches Stadion, today: Frankenstadion)
Max-Morlock-Platz

(F) Zeppelin Field, Zeppelin Grandstand
(Zeppelinfeld, Zeppelintribüne)
Beuthener Straße

(G) Luitpold Arena
(Luitpoldarena, Luitpoldhain)
An der Ehrenhalle

(H) March Field
(Märzfeld)
Langwasser, nearby Langwassersee

(I) March Field Railway Station
(Bahnhof Märzfeld)
Langwasser, Thomas-Mann-Straße

(J) Camp Area
(Lagergelände)
Today: Langwasser district